May 5   Orange Crowned, Black + White Warbler, Nashville Warbler, Black Throated Green Warbler, Chewink, Solitary Vireo + Great Blue Heron. Black duck 5 young. Red Shouldered Hawk and Savannah Sparrow

May 6   Baltimore Oriole, Scarlet Tanager, Rose Breasted Grosbeak - Catbird, Brown Thrasher, Chimney Swift, Yellow Warbler

" 7   Least Flycatcher

" 12   Bobolink, Spotted Sandpiper, Maryland Yellow Throat, Wilson Thrush, Night Heron, Green Heron, Chestnut Sided Warbler, Coopers Hawk.

" 13   House Wren, Kingbird - (Canadian Goose 7 young)

June 2   Purple Martin (2)

" 17   Ruby Throated Humming Bird

" 4   Yellow Rumped Warbler

" 8   Quail (2)   Three young Bucks Deer in our lower meadow.

Dec 15   (11) Evening Grosbeaks.   1946

1946

Feb 3   Sharp Shinned Hawk (killed on feeding box tree)

Mch 8   Song Sparrow, Blue Birds, Red Wings, Killdeer, Robins, Grackles.

" 9   7 Geese - Red Shouldered Hawk - Black Ducks.

" 16   White Billed Swallows - Hooded Merganser (8) Phoebe, Woodcock.

" 17   Flicker (Hicheran) Mourning Dove, Great Northern Shrike.

" 23   Meadow Lark, Cowbird-

April 8   Field Sparrow

" 13   Hood Winter Sparrow Hawks

" 14   Ruby Crowned Kinglet - Purple Finches

" 19   Chipping Sparrow, Barn Swallows + Myrtle Warbler - Swamp Sparrow

" 27   Pine Warbler, Chimney Swift

" 28   Solitary Vireo

May 3   White Throated Sparrow

" 4   Least Flycatcher, Baltimore Oriole, House Wren, Wood Thrush, Chewink, Brown Thrasher

" 10   Kingbird, Grey bird

" 11   Bobolink - White Crowned Sparrow, Catbird, Yellow Warbler, Black + White Warbler, Green Heron, Maryland Yellow Throat, Black Throated Green Warbler, Chestnut Sided Warbler, Scarlet Tanager, Wilson Thrush, Black Billed Cuckoo.

" 12   Rose Breasted Grosbeak, Red Start, Canadian Warbler, Magnolia Warbler, Red Eyed Vireo Nashville Warbler.

" 24   Ruby Throated Hummingbird, Night Hawk.

Nov 16   Fox Sparrow

1947

Jan 4   Purple Finch

" 5   Evening Grosbeaks (8)

" 18   Robin (1)

Feb 15   Red Shouldered Hawk

" 16   Sharp Shinned Hawk - (killed in feeding box tree)

Mch 8   Robins (300 Red Polls at feeding station)

" 9   Bluebird (   ) Bald Eagle. (10 Geese returned to 5/4 1 here) Red Winged Blackbird.

Buck + Doe
Seen beyond Peterseen
July 5 1945

Hylas in Wayland 3/16
46

1st Colarogus
April 27th

34° June 1st

Listened to Woodcock
singing in Wayland

Ice on Pond - mail ...
Mach 18th

Geese with 7 young
5/3 46

All three children
here X mas Day -
beautiful Skating.

The Bending Moment

The Bending Moment

D'Anne Bodman, *words*

Nancy Roberts, *photographs*

NIGHTWOOD PRESS

Carlisle, Massachusetts

❐

We would like to thank the following people for responding to our manuscript: Harvey Nosowitz, Paul Callahan, Mary Egan, Rene Stawicki, Helen Lyons, April Stone, Parrish Dobson, Katharine Bell, Weezie Petrie, Debbie Dawson, W.W., and Alan Aronie.

A special thanks to Miranda Hersey Kniffen for her intuition and perspicacity.

And to Roland Pease for his guidance and generous support.

First Edition published in 1998 by
NIGHTWOOD PRESS
Carlisle, Massachusetts

Library of Congress Catalog Card Number: 98-091613

ISBN 0-9665609-1-4

ISBN 0-9665609-0-6 (soft)

FIRST EDITION
Printed in the United States of America

□

For Clare, Amy Louise, Owen, and Sydney
Always building

I began photographing D'Anne's house on a hot August day in 1995. I wanted to document the existing house before the reconstruction began. I returned several times during the following fall, winter, and spring to record the changes in the structures. These pictures are about the rebirth of a house. They are also about my responses to the spaces, light, and surrounding landscape. I hope these images tell a story and also suggest other meanings and memories.

– N.R.

Through the benevolence of family and friends I had the opportunity to buy an old house on an extraordinary piece of property. The events and circumstances leading to the purchase seem to me even now miraculous and destined. I still wake up many mornings expecting someone to tell me to pack my bags, time to go home. To live in a place you have only imagined or visited in short glimpses of summer is to finally be where you can picture yourself. To make an image your home is to both arrive and return, remember and make new.

The house was at one time owned by a man who was an amateur naturalist. On his closet doors are recorded the birds he sighted, first asparagus and apple blossoms, weather, amount of snow and ice, storms, and trees lost from the late thirties through early seventies.

When the house was undergoing renovation, it occurred to me to keep my own record of the surroundings and what was taking place. I asked my good friend Nancy Roberts to photograph the various stages and thought I would keep some kind of journal visiting the site everyday. Instead, when I was able to sit down and write, it was always poems, and the spaces being created and framed were as much internal as external. Changing the view you change the landscape. Everything we make reinvents us.

– D.B.

The single most important principle for the strong design of structures is called "the bending moment."

Basically, a moment in engineering parlance is the principle of the lever. If you want to tighten a bolt, you can hold a wrench close to the bolt or you could grab the wrench at the end. The end of the wrench gives you more advantage. The distance at which a force acts influences the outcome. That is the principle of the moment.

Source: http://user.icx.net/~richarda/engineering.html

Epilogue

He calls. He says, tell me you haven't gone away.
Tell me about your house. I know it is beautiful. I
remember the first crocuses. Tell me when you will
come next. I will come tomorrow. I will come. I
say, I will not come, next. I cannot come.

My house is beautiful. All day a great and constant
hum. Friends come to dinner. Their children dance
on the patio. We are upside down, swinging, out
from under, swinging
in the sky
beyond

"You write, and write, and write."

The Bending Moment

Sleeping Lady

Sometimes called Beauty

The shape of distance

A woman

Softly we move while unseen
deer scatter the empty field

We stand looking past corners
light as winter
through open walls
breathing soundless

It has begun to snow beyond

windows still to be made

In the distance

silk black crow

cuts across the sky

Your dark lashes catching snow

To see and taste again
strawberries, so expensive early spring
when we ordered them anyway, even the cream
an extravagance

I would make an extravagant meal, nuts and cheeses
you say, not spring yet, not so costly as those strawberries
staining the bowl with their unexpected sweetness

When she folds the sheets her hands know what to do. Each crease careful and deliberate, the way she had once been taught to stitch bandages. Any stray thread might disturb the wound. She smoothes the sheets until edges are perfect seams, erasing any thoughtlessness. White as milk, straight as paper. Later, opened and spread upon the bed, her son will dream of banquets

Do we decide

when there is music

or do we wait for

that perfect turning

Above our voices

clouds flash the sun

between long sighs

of wind or my blood

Glass Flowers

Who could believe anything so perfect could be made by men.
The tools simple. To render what we see exactly, the particular of
each petal, leaf, root, stem. The most daring belief, a beautiful
heresy, uniqueness can be preserved. Like the night you rowed the
pond. Water shedding winter, slipping oars, faint lashes of trees.
No end to what the air could fashion. Stem and flower a breath
could shatter

Forgive me
wanting
length of day
expanse of night
cast of stars

It is just
we were enough
to light the house
and keep a fire breathing

all winter in a room
so small we could barely move

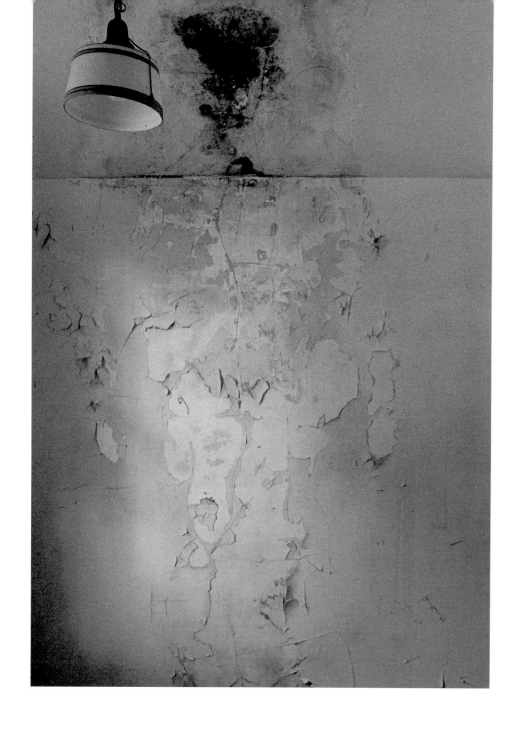

You ask me
why I want you
and we are still
close in that room
endless as day or night
where we come inside

They have closed off the house and you no longer
      reach the trees or stars as easily as breathing
All that we will see again is framed against
      other possibilities
Only the balconies remain to dream

You have more to lose, you say
and I have more to give
      though none of it is necessary
like candlelight
      eloquent and unpredictable

They have closed off the house
      trading raw landscape for comfort
so as not to lose an easier place to occupy

Outside the afternoon unaccountably changed
How do you measure what is not contained

So many gifts in a day
this last snow so abundant
the trees do not mind the burden
to wear silver and glass
and steal even the sun's glance

I will remember startlingly blue sky
each crow, deer, or snow goose
breaking winter's absence
with only their singleness

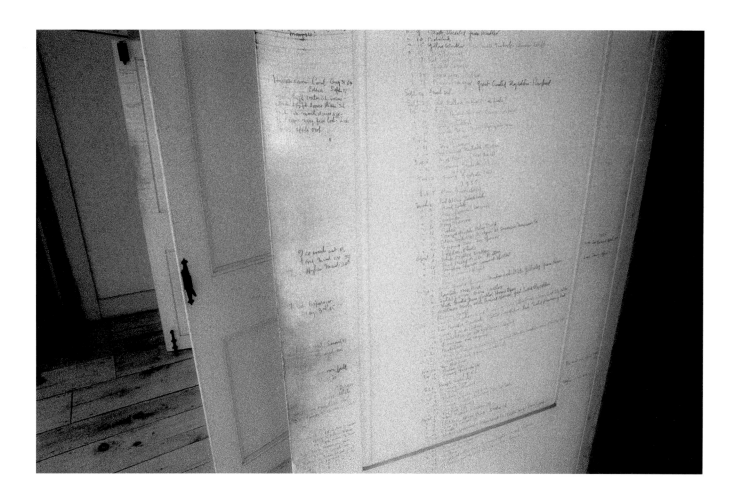

amid the jays. Suddenly, slivers of light strewn like seeds on the snow. First

        the sky above the pond turns silver then it is gold then it is

white again. The birds are gone and the clouds lift a red wing

     over the trees

Come and see
a poem waiting
to be written

The field has turned
to sky
billows white
erasing trees and pond
more wordless than
snow

                  All that we know
                  to be there
                  cannot be seen

We stand on the porch
waiting for field
or poem
gathering silence

Suddenly
even the weather
cannot let go of winter

I am wearing
all of the clothes
I had put away

I have not seen for
weeks your jacket
or cap (which secretly I have always wanted to wear)

my first image of you
and how the first poem began
Is this the last
I will write you

Geese. "Like a checkmark in the sky." Exactly right. To come by words

But you were only talking
always
only talk

The symmetry of geese
unexpected
rising between

to check the distance

What would I not

have given you

mock orange, wild rose,

mountain laurel

lasting day after

day you didn't come

You have given me back

the words I gave

as if they were names

of birds

you never expected to see

what trick of sun

after frost

gives back the sweetness

of the meadow

as if even now

it could be summer

and grass curled like wood shavings

steeps the air

until I cross the field

(where I brought you a drink)

to find a clearing

Nothing is
what I thought
Even your voice
when you spoke to me
was only
your voice

You were right
everything is what it is
there is no mistaking
the shape of wood
and the light
came from the glass
not the tree
or its smoothness

What seemed so large in winter
was only nakedness
and does not stay that way
for long

Rain

not snow

Rain

one loose bead

at a time

falls

from branches

already bare

I thought it was my body speaking, what it knows and wants, what it has never known can be. I thought I could never speak, except in your body, answer all your questions. But it is untold, no matter my deftness, unravelling of tongue. Untold, untold I must tell you again

The moon is a rose he says.

My last thought, my first thought.

Above speaking nights

a circle of stones.

The moon a rose

he says unfolding

Sweep of blooming sky

softer than a name

what are the chances
    of misunderstanding
    evening
    lit air of summer
    hovering invisible
    as fireflies

When you spoke about your father and the grapes he couldn't let you resist, you remember, more than their fragrant ripeness, his pleasure. Your face streaming with sweet juice, driving a dangerous load that any moment could go out of control. I see you now, still carrying these tons of grapes, willing and tireless because they can be made into wine. Yet, you laugh ungrudgingly while others eat the fruit, open your mouth to taste their joy

I thought I could tell

which was more beautiful

the sound made or the sound

not made

until yesterday

hidden in uncut grass

I could hear both

The woman is the Fall. No wind
      but the blood in her ears. She had cut her
      hair, put on a dress, begun to
stumble. The skirt failed to rise
          like a parachute, instead follows bend of waist,
    line of legs. Like a dive. There
is no scream. Her body
     is grace, unsuspended

Your father's wine jug, raffia covered, like those other jugs of village wine in places I did not know you. The wine unmistakable, in bars without names, red and young as evenings unfinished by the sea. I might have known you, sleeping on the ferry deck, a bench in some harbor town, if you slept then, or in a marketplace buying nothing, carrying only stories. Even now, waiting with your daughter for the stories they cannot help but tell you, your lean frame in motion in some wilder place, I taste the days in between the lives we made. How long can I drink?

What is it to see
the lake and her eyes
the same color
as if somehow
you have looked closely
and discovered a secret
blue-green lake inside her

It is unknowing
to mistake one shape
for another
until there is only space

How do you describe a face? When it is gone.

From the side, the back of the neck, walking

into the sun. The way light falls and changes.

The way light comes from skin. The distance

before he turns and sees you. A face you see

everywhere. In unfamiliar cars and streets.

For a moment. Before you remember. A face

inexplicably changed

Made possible in part by a 1997 Regional Fellowship for Visual Artists Domestic Life Interpreted Award to Nancy P. Roberts, administered by the New England Foundation for the Arts and funded by the Polaroid Foundation, the Massachusetts Cultural Council, the New England Foundation for the Arts, and the National Endowment for the Arts.

This book was designed by Jennie R. Bush, Books By Design Inc., Somerville, Massachusetts, printed by The Stinehour Press, Lunenburg, Vermont, and bound by New Hampshire Bindery, Concord, New Hampshire. The type face is Bembo. The photographs print as duotones. The paper is Warren's Lustro Offset Enamel Dull, an acid free paper. The end leaves are Strathmore Pastelle.

1943

Dec 18. 43   11 Evening Grosbeaks - at feeding station.
                                        1944
Jan 15. 44   1 Mourning Dove.
Feb. 27.   21 of our geese returned - having been away since November 43
Mch 12 -   Song Sparrows - Red Winged Blackbirds,
"   18   Robin - Bluebird - Meadow Larks (Bedford) Grackles -
"   19   Rusty Blackbird (2)
"   25   White Bellied Swallow - Fox Sparrow - Flicker Blackbirds - Mourning Dove .
"   26   Cowbird, Phoebe, Red Shouldered Hawk - Killdeer - (2) Buffle Head Ducks
April 7   Meadowlarks - Wood Ducks.
"   8   Bittern
"   15   Field Sparrow - Kingfisher (3) Hooded Mergansers .
"   21   First Hylas of the year.
"   22   Chipping Sparrow - Vesper Sparrow - Barn Swallow - Pine Warbler - Yellow Palm Warbler
              Yellow Rumped Warbler
"   23   Ruby Crowned Kinglet
"   30   Purple Finch (singing) - Heron Yellow Legs.
May 1.   Black & White Warbler
"   6   Black Throated Green Warbler - Least Flycatcher - Yellow Warbler - House Wren - Redstart . Baltimore Oriole, Veery Bird
              Savannah Sparrow, Maryland Yellow Throat, Chestnut Sided Warbler, Ovenbird - Kingbird. Bobolink -
              Nashville Warbler
May 7.   Rose Breasted Grosbeak - Cat Bird - Chimney Swifts - Brown Thrasher - Greenthorn - Wood Thrush.
              Evening Grosbeak .
May 8   Red Eyed Vireo - Night Heron
"   13   Scarlet Tanager - Veery Thrush, Black Billed Cuckoo.
"   26   Catbird (?)
"   27   Night Hawk - Prairie Warbler
"   28   Crested Flycatcher
June 3   Whip poor will -
                                        1945
Jan 27   Screech Owl -
Feb 17   1 Sharp Shinned Hawk - (killed a chickadee in bird feeding station - so I killed him!)
Mch 3.   Song Sparrow (singing)   Bluebird.
"   10   Red Winged Blackbirds -
"   11   Meadowlarks - Grackles
"   16   Robins
"   17   Black Ducks - Hooded Mergansers - Red Shouldered Hawk - (11 geese)
"   18   White Breasted Swallows, Phoebe - Fox Sparrows - Rusty Blackbirds - Buffle Heads (5)
"   24   Cowbirds - Mourning Dove
"   26   Killdeer
April 1   Chipping Sparrows - Flicker (Yellow??)
"   2   Purple Finch (singing)
"   7   Field Sparrow - Ruby Crowned Kinglet - Wood Duck - Marsh Hawk
"   8   Vesper Sparrow - Swamp Sparrow - Pine Warbler - Palm Warbler - Yellow Rumped Warbler
"   14   Belted Kingfisher, Osprey, Hermit Thrush (singing)
"   18   Whitewand - Barn Swallows
"   28   White Throated Sparrow - Bittern
May 5   Cat Bird - Black & White Warbler - Nashville Warbler - Black Throated Green Warbler
              Ovenbird - Solitary Vireo -

Mch 19   4° above Zero 44
9" Snow march 20th 44

Pond clear of ice - April 7th

Hylas - April 21

1st Asparagus - may 6th

1st Sweet Corn July 21. 44

17" Snow fall - Feb 8th 45

Out in Canoe Mch 18
pond 3/4 clear of ice
Hylas Mch 25th

1st Asparagus
April 15th 45

Rose - Bob + Pete all
here for lunch April 30 44
photo was taken of them then
for Xmas Card 44

Apple Blossoms out
full May 14 44 (early)

Killing frost - May 19
(26°) Lost all apples -

7 geese returned
on Mch 9th 45

Plum tree in bloom April 13
Shad Bush
+ Apple Blossoms out
April 14 45